SAMSUNG
Galaxy S24

Samsung Galaxy S24 User Guide

Tips, and Tricks for Beginners and Advanced Users Helps to Mastery, and Attaos enable Optimum User Experience & Lots More

Nolan White

Table of Content

Introduction

The Samsung Galaxy S24 series represents the latest evolution in Samsung's long and storied line of premium smartphones. Unveiled with much fanfare in 2024, this series continues Samsung's tradition of pushing the envelope in mobile technology, design, and user experience. Comprising the Galaxy S24, S24+, and S24 Ultra, this lineup offers a range of options catering to various user needs, from the standard model's solid performance and compact design to the Ultra's cutting-edge technology and professional-grade photography capabilities.

CHAPTER 1

Overview of the Samsung Galaxy S24 Series

The Galaxy S24 series is Samsung's bold statement in the smartphone market, showcasing its commitment to innovation, luxury, and unparalleled functionality. Each model in the series has been designed with precision, embodying elegance with their sleek frames, dynamic AMOLED displays, and a robust build quality that has become synonymous with Samsung's flagship offerings.

- **Galaxy S24:** The entry-level model of the series doesn't skimp on features. It boasts a powerful new chipset, an advanced camera system for stunning photography, and a high-refresh-rate display for smooth visuals. Its compact form factor makes it an ideal choice for users who prefer a more manageable device without compromising on performance.

- **Galaxy S24+:** Building on the foundation of the S24, the Plus model offers enhanced features, including a larger screen for immersive viewing experiences, a bigger battery for extended use, and additional camera capabilities. It strikes a perfect balance between functionality and portability, catering to users looking for that extra edge in their smartphone experience.

- **Galaxy S24 Ultra:** The pinnacle of Samsung's smartphone technology, the S24 Ultra is a powerhouse designed for those who demand the best. With a state-of-the-art camera system featuring unprecedented zoom and clarity, a massive display that brings content to life, and a battery that keeps up with even the most demanding users, the Ultra is more than just a phone; it's a professional-grade camera, a gaming device, and a productivity powerhouse, all rolled into one.

What's New in 2024

The 2024 iteration of Samsung's flagship series introduces several key advancements that set new standards in the smartphone industry:

- **Enhanced AI Integration:** In collaboration with Google, Samsung has deeply integrated AI across the S24 series, offering smarter, context-aware suggestions, enhanced computational photography, and real-time language translation, making the Galaxy S24 series not just faster but more intuitive.

- **Revolutionary Camera Capabilities:** The S24 series brings professional-grade photography to your pocket. The S24 Ultra, in particular, features a groundbreaking 200MP sensor, offering unprecedented detail and clarity. Enhanced night mode, astrophotography capabilities, and improved optical zoom are just the tip of the iceberg, with AI enhancements pushing the boundaries of what's possible with a smartphone camera.

- **Eco-friendly Manufacturing:** Samsung has made significant strides in sustainability, utilizing recycled materials in the construction of the S24 series and adopting more eco-friendly manufacturing processes. This commitment to the environment is a key feature of the 2024 lineup, reducing the carbon footprint without compromising on quality or performance.

- **Next-generation Connectivity:** With the introduction of Wi-Fi 6E and improved 5G capabilities, the Galaxy S24 series offers faster, more reliable connections, ensuring that users stay connected no matter where they are. Whether streaming, gaming, or working remotely, the S24 series is equipped to handle high-bandwidth applications with ease.

- **Improved Display Technology:** The S24 series' displays are brighter, more vibrant, and more energy-efficient than ever before. With adaptive refresh rates up to 120Hz, users can enjoy smooth scrolling and fluid motion in games and apps, all while conserving battery life.

- **Customizable Software Experience:** Samsung's One UI has been further refined, offering more customization options, improved security features, and seamless integration with the Samsung ecosystem of devices. The S24 series is not just about powerful hardware; it's about creating a cohesive, user-centric experience across all devices.

CHAPTER 2

Design and Build

The Samsung Galaxy S24 series, including the Galaxy S24, S24+, and S24 Ultra, showcases Samsung's commitment to pioneering not just the technological aspects of their devices but also their physical design and construction. This section explores the meticulous attention to detail in the physical dimensions, weight, aesthetics, choice of materials, color options, and the series' resilience to water and dust.

Physical Dimensions and Weight Comparison

The Galaxy S24 series offers a range of sizes to cater to various user preferences and needs. The standard S24 model is the most compact, designed for ease of use with one hand, reflecting a balance between screen size and portability. The S24+ offers a slightly larger display and overall footprint, targeting users who consume a lot of media on their devices but still value a sleek form factor. The S24 Ultra stands at the pinnacle, with its substantial screen and body designed for maximum screen real estate and the integration of advanced technology, especially in its camera system.

Each model's weight is carefully calibrated to balance its larger screen and battery capacity with the need for a comfortable hand feel and usability over extended periods. Advanced materials play a critical role in achieving this balance, allowing for a reduction in weight without compromising durability.

- Design Aesthetics: Materials and Color Options

Samsung has long been celebrated for its design innovation, and the Galaxy S24 series is no exception. The company continues to push the boundaries of smartphone design with a sophisticated blend of glass and metal, creating a premium look and feel. The use of Gorilla Glass Victus in the series promises enhanced durability against drops and scratches, while the choice of an aluminum or stainless steel frame (depending on the model) provides structural integrity and a luxurious touch.

The color palette for the S24 series is both diverse and elegant, offering options that range from classic hues to more vibrant and experimental tones. This variety ensures that there's a style to suit every taste, from understated elegance to bold statements. The finish on each device, whether matte or glossy, is selected to enhance the chosen color, creating a sophisticated aesthetic that complements its premium design.

- **Water and Dust Resistance Ratings:** The Galaxy S24 series is built to withstand the elements, featuring IP68 water and dust resistance across all models. This rating ensures that each device can be submerged in up to 1.5 meters of freshwater for up to

30 minutes without sustaining damage. Dust resistance is equally robust, providing protection against dust ingress that could otherwise compromise the device's performance.

This resilience makes the Galaxy S24 series ideal for a wide range of environments and activities, from outdoor adventures to everyday spills and mishaps. It's a testament to Samsung's commitment to creating devices that are not only technologically advanced but also durable and reliable under various conditions.

In crafting the Galaxy S24 series, Samsung has once again set a benchmark for smartphone design and build quality. From their ergonomic dimensions and lightweight yet durable construction to their refined aesthetics and resilience against water and dust, these devices are designed to meet the demands of modern users who seek a perfect blend of style, functionality, and durability. The careful consideration of materials, colors, and protective features reflects Samsung's deep understanding of its users' needs and its dedication to exceeding those expectations with every new release.

CHAPTER 3

Display Technology

The Samsung Galaxy S24 series epitomizes the pinnacle of smartphone display technology, incorporating cutting-edge advancements to offer users an unparalleled viewing experience. This section delves into the nuances of the series' display capabilities, focusing on screen size and resolution, Dynamic AMOLED 2X technology, and the key attributes of brightness, color accuracy, and viewing angles.

Screen Size and Resolution Differences

The Galaxy S24 series showcases a diverse range of screen sizes and resolutions tailored to different user preferences and needs. The standard Galaxy S24 model features a compact screen designed for one-handed use without compromising on clarity or detail, making it ideal for everyday tasks and multimedia consumption. The S24+ scales up the display size, offering a more immersive viewing experience suitable for video streaming, gaming, and productivity tasks that benefit from additional screen real estate.

At the apex of the series, the Galaxy S24 Ultra boasts the largest and most high-resolution display. This mammoth screen is not just about size; it offers an unparalleled pixel density, ensuring that images and text are rendered with crisp clarity, enhancing the viewing experience for photography, high-definition videos, and intricate graphical content.

Each model's resolution is meticulously calibrated to balance sharpness, power consumption, and performance, ensuring that from the standard S24 to the Ultra, users enjoy a visually stunning experience optimized for their device's specific capabilities and design.

Dynamic AMOLED 2X Technology

Dynamic AMOLED 2X, the proprietary display technology developed by Samsung, stands at the heart of the Galaxy S24 series' exceptional display performance. This technology represents a significant leap forward in display capabilities, offering vibrant colors, deep blacks, and an incredible contrast ratio that makes every image pop with life-like detail.

The "2X" denotes an enhanced version of Samsung's already impressive AMOLED displays, with improvements in brightness, energy efficiency, and color fidelity. This technology allows the S24 series displays to adapt dynamically to different lighting conditions, ensuring that the screen remains perfectly visible and stunningly vibrant, whether in direct sunlight or a dimly lit room.

One of the hallmark features of Dynamic AMOLED 2X is its reduced blue light emission, which minimizes eye strain during prolonged use without affecting the display's color accuracy. This makes the

Galaxy S24 series not only easier on the eyes but also one of the most environmentally friendly displays on the market, further cementing Samsung's commitment to sustainability and user well-being.

Brightness, Color Accuracy, and Viewing Angles

Brightness, color accuracy, and viewing angles are critical factors that define the quality of a smartphone display, and the Galaxy S24 series excels in each of these areas. The series features displays capable of achieving peak brightness levels that surpass those of its predecessors and competitors, ensuring excellent visibility in all lighting conditions. This high brightness capability is coupled with an intelligent auto-brightness adjustment feature, which optimizes the screen's luminance based on the ambient light, enhancing both user comfort and battery efficiency.

Color accuracy is another area where the Galaxy S24 series shines, thanks to the sophisticated calibration of its Dynamic AMOLED 2X displays. These screens cover a wide color spectrum, including 100% of the DCI-P3 color space, which is a standard in the film industry for color accuracy. As a result, colors are rendered with exceptional fidelity, bringing images and videos to life with vibrant hues and nuanced shades that mirror reality.

The viewing angles on the Galaxy S24 series displays are equally impressive, maintaining consistent color and brightness even when viewed from sharp angles. This is particularly beneficial when sharing content on your screen with others, ensuring that everyone gets the same high-quality viewing experience regardless of their position relative to the device.

CHAPTER 4

Performance and Hardware

The Samsung Galaxy S24 series stands as a testament to the relentless pursuit of technological excellence, offering unparalleled performance and hardware specifications that cater to the needs of even the most demanding users. From its state-of-the-art chipset to versatile storage options and exceptional battery life, each aspect of the series' hardware has been meticulously designed to push the boundaries of what's possible with a smartphone.

Chipset Specifications: Snapdragon 8 Gen 3

At the core of the Galaxy S24 series' exceptional performance lies the Snapdragon 8 Gen 3 chipset, the latest and most powerful processor from Qualcomm. This chipset represents a significant leap forward in processing power, efficiency, and AI capabilities, setting a new benchmark for smartphone performance.

Built on an advanced 5nm process technology, the Snapdragon 8 Gen 3 provides substantial improvements in CPU and GPU performance compared to its predecessor, ensuring smooth, lag-free experiences across gaming, multimedia consumption, and day-to-day tasks. The chipset's enhanced AI engine drives smarter, more personalized experiences, enabling features such as real-time language translation, advanced image processing, and predictive app loading to make the user experience more seamless than ever.

Moreover, the Snapdragon 8 Gen 3 includes an integrated 5G modem, offering faster, more reliable connections with improved energy efficiency. This integration ensures that the Galaxy S24 series is not only future-proofed for the next generation of mobile networks but also optimized for lower power consumption, enhancing battery life even with heavy 5G usage.

RAM and Storage Options

Understanding that users have diverse needs, the Galaxy S24 series offers a wide range of RAM and storage configurations to suit various preferences and requirements. The series starts with a base model equipped with 8GB of RAM, catering to the everyday needs of the average user, and scales up to 16GB for the Ultra model, designed for power users who demand the highest level of multitasking and performance.

Storage options are equally flexible, with the base model offering 128GB of onboard storage, ensuring ample space for apps, photos, and media. For users with higher storage needs, the series provides options up to 1TB, allowing for the storage of extensive media libraries, large apps, and games without the need for constant management of storage space.

Samsung has also maintained its commitment to user convenience by including expandable storage options in the Galaxy S24 series, a feature increasingly rare in high-end smartphones. This allows users to easily increase their storage capacity through microSD cards, providing flexibility and ensuring that storage needs are always met.

Battery Life and Charging Capabilities

Battery life and charging capabilities are critical components of the user experience, and the Galaxy S24 series excels in both areas. Each model in the series features a large-capacity battery designed to last through a full day of heavy usage, with the Ultra model equipped with an even larger battery to accommodate its more power-intensive features.

The series supports fast charging, both wired and wireless, enabling users to quickly recharge their devices and minimize downtime. Samsung has further refined its charging technology to offer faster charging speeds without compromising battery health, ensuring that the Galaxy S24 series' batteries maintain their capacity over time.

Additionally, the series features reverse wireless charging, allowing users to charge other devices, such as earbuds or smartwatches, directly from their smartphones. This feature underscores Samsung's vision of a seamlessly integrated ecosystem of devices, providing added convenience for users on the go.

CHAPTER 5

Camera Systems

The camera systems of the Samsung Galaxy S24 series embody Samsung's commitment to pushing the boundaries of mobile photography, combining advanced hardware with sophisticated software to cater to photographers of all levels. From the versatile camera setups across the S24, S24+, and S24 Ultra to the inclusion of cutting-edge AI-driven photography enhancements, these devices are designed to capture stunning images and videos in any condition.

Overview of Camera Specifications

The Galaxy S24 series features a multi-lens camera system designed to offer unparalleled versatility and quality in mobile photography. The standard S24 model includes a triple camera setup, comprising a high-resolution main sensor, an ultra-wide lens for capturing expansive scenes, and a telephoto lens for detailed zoom shots. This configuration ensures users can tackle a wide range of photographic scenarios, from vast landscapes to detailed portraits.

The S24+ builds upon the foundation of the S24, offering enhanced optical zoom capabilities and larger sensor sizes for improved low-light performance. The addition of dedicated sensors for depth perception and enhanced optical image stabilization (OIS) further refines the photographic output, providing sharper images and smoother video capture.

At the pinnacle of the series, the S24 Ultra boasts the most advanced camera system, featuring a groundbreaking primary sensor that offers unprecedented resolution and clarity. The Ultra model also includes a periscope-style telephoto lens capable of delivering significant optical zoom, allowing for detailed shots of distant subjects without loss of quality. Advanced features such as Laser AF (Auto Focus) and enhanced night mode capabilities further distinguish the Ultra's camera system, making it a benchmark for mobile photography.

Comparison of Camera Capabilities: S24 vs. S24+ vs. S24 Ultra

While all models within the Galaxy S24 series are equipped with impressive camera systems, key differences in their capabilities cater to varying user needs and preferences. The standard S24 offers a solid all-around photography experience suitable for most users, with its triple lens setup providing flexibility in shot composition and a strong balance between image quality and functionality.

The S24+ introduces improvements primarily in the realms of zoom and low-light photography, catering to users who demand a bit more from their mobile photography experience. The enhanced sensors and

OIS make it a more capable device for capturing detailed images in a wider range of lighting conditions.

The S24 Ultra is targeted at photography enthusiasts and professionals who require the highest level of performance from their smartphone camera. Its superior resolution, zoom capabilities, and support for advanced photography modes, such as manual controls and RAW image capture, make it a true standout. The Ultra's camera system rivals that of dedicated cameras, offering creative possibilities previously unthinkable on a smartphone.

Advanced Photography Features and AI Enhancements

Across the Galaxy S24 series, Samsung has integrated a suite of advanced photography features and AI enhancements that elevate the mobile photography experience. AI-driven scene optimization automatically adjusts camera settings to suit the subject and lighting conditions, ensuring optimal exposure and color accuracy without manual adjustments.

Night mode has been significantly improved, with AI algorithms working to reduce noise and enhance detail in low-light conditions, producing clear, vibrant images that are rich in detail. Portrait mode benefits from AI segmentation technology, accurately separating subjects from their background for professional-looking bokeh effects.

The S24 series also introduces innovative features such as Single Take, which captures a series of photos and videos with a single press of the shutter button, and Director's View for dynamic video recording from multiple lenses simultaneously. AI object eraser allows users to remove unwanted elements from their photos post-capture, showcasing the powerful integration of AI into the photography workflow.

CHAPTER 6

Software and User Experience

The Samsung Galaxy S24 series epitomizes the seamless integration of high-end hardware with sophisticated software, offering a user experience that is both intuitive and enriching. Central to this experience is Samsung's One UI, built on the latest Android platform, which brings exclusive software features, extensive customizations, and AI-powered innovations to the forefront, significantly enhanced by Samsung's collaboration with Google.

Operating System and UI: One UI

One UI, Samsung's custom interface layered on top of the Android operating system, is designed with focus, convenience, and efficiency in mind. With each iteration, One UI has become more refined, offering a clean, user-friendly interface that enhances the overall user experience on Galaxy devices. The version of One UI on the Galaxy S24 series introduces a slew of optimizations and enhancements that leverage the powerful hardware of the S24, S24+, and S24 Ultra, providing a smooth, responsive experience that users have come to expect from Samsung.

Key to One UI's appeal is its ability to offer a consistent experience across Samsung devices, whether smartphones, tablets, or wearables. This ecosystem integration ensures that users enjoy a seamless transition between devices, with shared services and synchronized data. One UI's design language, with its intuitive controls, customizable themes, and thoughtful layout, further enhances usability, making technology accessible to a broader range of users.

Exclusive Software Features and Customizations

Samsung Galaxy S24 series comes packed with exclusive software features that set it apart from the competition. Edge Panels, for instance, offer quick access to apps, tools, and contacts with just a swipe from the screen's edge, enhancing multitasking and efficiency. Samsung DeX, another standout feature, transforms the smartphone into a desktop computing experience when connected to a monitor, with a mouse and keyboard, offering unparalleled productivity on the go.

Customization is another cornerstone of the Galaxy S24 series experience. From AOD (Always On Display) options that allow users to see information at a glance without waking the phone to extensive theme and icon packs available in the Galaxy Store, users can tailor their devices to reflect their personal style and preferences.

One UI also integrates comprehensive privacy and security features, including Secure Folder for encrypting personal data and Samsung Knox for defense-grade security right from the chip level, ensuring that users' data and privacy are protected.

AI-Powered Innovations and Google Partnership Highlights

The integration of AI across the Galaxy S24 series enriches the user experience with smart features that anticipate and respond to user needs. Bixby, Samsung's AI assistant, offers voice control, Bixby Routines for automating tasks based on time of day or location, and Bixby Vision for augmented reality experiences. These AI-powered features simplify interactions and enhance productivity, making the Galaxy S24 series not just a tool but a proactive assistant in users' daily lives.

Samsung's partnership with Google brings additional AI-powered innovations to the S24 series, leveraging Google's expertise in AI and machine learning to enhance the software experience. Google Duo live sharing, for instance, allows users to share their screen during video calls, enhancing collaboration and connectivity. Integration with Google's ecosystem, including Maps, Photos, and Assistant, ensures that Galaxy S24 users have access to the best services and apps, optimized for their devices.

Furthermore, this partnership has led to exclusive features like the improved Google Discover feed, direct access to Google's wide array of services from the home screen, and enhanced security and privacy controls that give users more power over their data.

CHAPTER 7

Connectivity and Network Support

The Samsung Galaxy S24 series represents the zenith of smartphone connectivity and network support, offering users a wide range of advanced options to stay connected. These features are not just about maintaining calls or browsing the internet; they are about ensuring seamless, high-speed connectivity for everything from streaming content to playing online games, and even controlling smart home devices. Let's delve into the specifics.

5G, Wi-Fi 6/6E, and Bluetooth 5.0 Capabilities

5G Connectivity: The Galaxy S24 series comes equipped with the latest in cellular technology, 5G, providing users with unprecedented download and upload speeds. This leap in connectivity is not merely an incremental improvement; it's transformative, enabling near-instantaneous data transfer, high-quality video streaming without buffering, and ultra-responsive online gaming. 5G also opens up new possibilities for augmented and virtual reality applications, making the Galaxy S24 series future-proof in the rapidly evolving digital landscape.

- **Wi-Fi 6/6E Support:** Alongside 5G, the Galaxy S24 series supports Wi-Fi 6 and 6E, the latest standards in wireless networking. These technologies offer faster speeds, reduced latency, and greater capacity, allowing more devices to connect to the network without impacting performance. Wi-Fi 6/6E ensures that whether you're at home or in a crowded public space, your S24 device will deliver a stable and swift internet connection, making everything from video conferencing to downloading large files more efficient.

- **Bluetooth 5.0:** To complement its cellular and Wi-Fi capabilities, the Galaxy S24 series incorporates Bluetooth 5.0, providing enhanced range, faster speeds, and more reliable connections to Bluetooth devices. This means better-quality audio streaming to wireless headphones, seamless connectivity to wearables like smartwatches and fitness trackers, and improved performance for gaming controllers. Bluetooth 5.0 also introduces capabilities for location services and IoT (Internet of Things) devices, making the S24 series a central hub for controlling smart home gadgets.

Dual SIM and eSIM Support

- **Dual SIM Functionality:** Recognizing the diverse needs of its users, Samsung has equipped the Galaxy S24 series with Dual SIM capabilities, allowing users to maintain two separate phone numbers or service plans on a single device. This feature is invaluable for travelers, business professionals, and anyone looking to separate work and personal communications. Dual SIM functionality offers flexibility in managing calls, texts, and data usage, enabling users to switch between SIMs effortlessly or use one for calls and texts and the other for data.

- **eSIM Support:** In addition to traditional SIM cards, the Galaxy S24 series supports eSIM technology, a game-changer in smartphone connectivity. An eSIM (embedded SIM) is a digital SIM that allows users to activate a cellular plan without the need for a physical SIM card. This facilitates easier switching between carriers, instant activation of mobile service, and the ability to use multiple phone numbers on the same device. eSIM support also frees up space inside the phone for other components, contributing to the sleek design of the S24 series.

In combination, the advanced connectivity and network support features of the Samsung Galaxy S24 series ensure that users can stay connected in more ways than ever before. The inclusion of 5G, Wi-Fi 6/6E, Bluetooth 5.0, Dual SIM, and eSIM technologies not only enhances the device's usability and flexibility but also positions the Galaxy S24 series at the forefront of the digital revolution, ready to meet the demands of today's hyper-connected world.

CHAPTER 8

Security Features

The Samsung Galaxy S24 series places a significant emphasis on security, integrating advanced features to protect users' data and privacy. In today's digital age, where smartphones are central to our personal and professional lives, ensuring the security of sensitive information is paramount. Samsung addresses this through biometric security measures and a robust security platform.

Fingerprint Sensors and Facial Recognition

Fingerprint Sensors: The Galaxy S24 series incorporates ultrasonic fingerprint sensors, a cutting-edge biometric security feature. Unlike traditional optical sensors, ultrasonic fingerprint sensors use sound waves to create a detailed 3D map of the user's fingerprint. This technology offers several advantages, including improved accuracy and the ability to read fingerprints through water or grease, ensuring consistent performance in various conditions. The sensor is embedded under the display, allowing for a seamless design without compromising on security or accessibility.

- **Facial Recognition:** Complementing the fingerprint sensor, the Galaxy S24 series also features sophisticated facial recognition technology. Using advanced algorithms and the front-facing camera, the device can quickly and accurately identify the registered user, providing a secure and convenient way to unlock the phone. Facial recognition in the S24 series is designed to adapt to changes in appearance, such as facial hair or glasses, ensuring reliable performance over time. Together, the fingerprint sensor and facial recognition offer users flexible and secure options for protecting their devices.

Samsung Knox Security Platform

- **Overview:** At the heart of the Galaxy S24 series' security features is the Samsung Knox security platform. Knox is a multi-layered security solution that protects the device at the hardware and software levels, safeguarding against malware, phishing, and other cyber threats. From the moment the device is powered on, Knox continuously monitors and protects the system from potential vulnerabilities, offering peace of mind to users.

- **Key Features:** Samsung Knox provides a comprehensive suite of security features, including Secure Folder, a private encrypted space where users can store sensitive files, apps, and data. Knox also supports secure boot and real-time kernel protection, preventing unauthorized software from compromising the device. For business users, Knox enables the separation of work and personal data, ensuring that sensitive corporate information remains secure and isolated from personal apps and content.

- **Enterprise Solutions:** Beyond individual security, Samsung Knox offers robust solutions for enterprise environments. Knox Manage, for example, allows IT administrators to remotely manage and secure Samsung devices within their organization, enforcing policies, deploying apps, and controlling access to data. Knox Platform for Enterprise goes even further, offering advanced controls for data encryption, network protection, and identity verification, making the Galaxy S24 series an ideal choice for businesses concerned with mobile security.

CHAPTER 9

Accessories and Compatibility

The Samsung Galaxy S24 series, with its cutting-edge design and advanced features, is complemented by a wide range of accessories and compatibility options. These not only enhance the functionality and durability of the devices but also integrate them into the broader ecosystem of wearables and smart home devices.

Cases, Screen Protectors, and Official Accessories

- **Cases and Screen Protectors:** Protecting the premium design and display of the Galaxy S24 series is paramount for users. Samsung offers a variety of cases and screen protectors tailored to fit each model perfectly. From clear cases that showcase the phone's design to rugged cases that provide maximum protection against drops, there's an option for every preference. Leather cases add a touch of elegance, while silicone cases offer a comfortable grip. Screen protectors, designed to adhere seamlessly to the curved displays, preserve the touch sensitivity and clarity of the screen, ensuring it remains free from scratches and cracks.

- **Official Accessories:** Beyond protection, Samsung enhances the Galaxy S24 series experience with official accessories that leverage the devices' capabilities. The S Pen, compatible with the Ultra model, enables precise input and creative expression. Wireless chargers and power banks ensure the devices are always powered, featuring fast charging capabilities. The Galaxy Buds series offer a seamless audio experience, with features like noise cancellation and ambient sound mode. Samsung DeX accessories transform the S24 into a desktop computing platform, proving the versatility of these smartphones.

Compatibility with Wearables and Smart Home Devices

- **Wearables:** The Galaxy S24 series is designed to work seamlessly with Samsung's range of wearable devices, including the Galaxy Watch and Galaxy Buds series. These wearables extend the functionality of the smartphones, allowing users to track their health metrics, control music playback, and even manage notifications and calls directly from their wrists or ears. The integration between the Galaxy S24 series and Samsung wearables is seamless, thanks to shared software features and a unified design language that enhances the user experience across devices.

- **Smart Home Devices:** As part of the broader Samsung ecosystem, the Galaxy S24 series can serve as a central hub for controlling a wide array of smart home devices. Through the SmartThings app, users can connect their smartphones to Samsung appliances, smart TVs, and third-party devices like smart lights, thermostats, and security cameras. This integration allows for the creation of routines and scenarios, automating tasks based on time of day or user presence. For example, lights can be set to turn off automatically when the user leaves home, or the TV can be paused when a call comes in on the Galaxy S24.

The compatibility with wearables and smart home devices underscores the Galaxy S24 series' role not just as smartphones, but as central components of a connected lifestyle. Whether through health and fitness tracking with wearables or home automation and control with SmartThings, the Galaxy S24 series offers users a cohesive and integrated experience that extends beyond the phone itself.

CHAPTER 10

Comparison with Competitors

The smartphone market is fiercely competitive, with each brand striving to outdo the others in terms of innovation, performance, and value. The Samsung Galaxy S24 series enters this arena with high expectations, boasting advanced features and specifications designed to challenge its closest rivals, namely the iPhone 14 from Apple and the Google Pixel 8.

How the S24 Series Stacks Up Against iPhone 14 and Google Pixel 8

- **Design and Display:** The Galaxy S24 series continues Samsung's tradition of sleek, premium design with Dynamic AMOLED 2X displays that offer vibrant colors, deep blacks, and high brightness levels. Compared to the iPhone 14's Super Retina

XDR display and the Google Pixel 8's OLED screen, the S24 offers a more customizable Always-On display and higher refresh rates, making for smoother scrolling and better gaming experiences.

- **Performance:** Powered by the Snapdragon 8 Gen 3 chipset, the Galaxy S24 series provides robust performance that rivals the A15 Bionic chip in the iPhone 14 and the custom Google Tensor chip in the Pixel 8. While all three devices offer smooth performance for everyday tasks and demanding applications, the S24's advanced cooling systems and AI capabilities might edge out in multitasking and AI-driven tasks.

- **Camera System:** The Galaxy S24 series boasts significant camera enhancements, especially in the Ultra model, with features like 200MP sensors and advanced zoom capabilities. While the iPhone 14 is known for its color accuracy and video stabilization and the Pixel 8 for its computational photography, the S24 series aims to offer a more versatile camera experience, potentially outperforming its rivals in zoom and low-light photography.

- **Software and Ecosystem:** The Galaxy S24 series runs on One UI, offering a customizable Android experience with added Samsung features. In contrast, the iPhone 14 offers a seamless but more closed ecosystem with iOS, and the Pixel 8 provides a stock Android experience with direct updates from Google. Each offers unique advantages: Samsung for customization, Apple for ecosystem integration, and Google for pure Android with AI enhancements.

- **Battery Life and Charging:** The S24 series aims to improve upon its predecessors' already impressive battery life and fast charging capabilities. While the iPhone 14 and Pixel 8 have made strides in battery efficiency, the S24's larger battery capacities and faster charging might give it an edge for power users.

Price-to-Performance Analysis

When evaluating the price-to-performance ratio, it's essential to consider the starting prices of these devices in relation to their hardware specifications, software features, and overall user experience. The Galaxy S24 series, with its advanced display technology, camera capabilities, and robust performance, offers competitive value, especially considering its base model's price compared to the iPhone 14 and Pixel 8.

The S24 Ultra, with its premium features, competes directly with the higher-priced iPhone 14 Pro Max and Pixel 8 Pro, offering a compelling alternative for users prioritizing photography and display quality. However, the value of software updates, ecosystem integration, and brand loyalty can significantly influence user preference and perceived value.

CHAPTER 11

Purchasing Options

The Samsung Galaxy S24 series, with its cutting-edge features and premium design, presents potential buyers with a variety of purchasing options. These options are designed to accommodate different user preferences and financial considerations, ensuring that the latest technology is accessible to a wide audience. Understanding the nuances of unlocked versus carrier models, along with the advantages of financing and trade-in programs, can help consumers make informed decisions that suit their needs and budgets.

Unlocked vs. Carrier Models

- **Unlocked Models:** Purchasing an unlocked Galaxy S24 means buying the device without any carrier tie-ins or contracts. This option offers several benefits, including the freedom to choose or switch between carriers at will, potentially leading to better service deals or coverage. Unlocked phones are not loaded with carrier-specific apps or bloatware, providing a cleaner, more streamlined user experience. Additionally, unlocked devices typically receive software updates more promptly since they don't require carrier approval. However, the upfront cost of an unlocked phone can be higher, as it doesn't benefit from carrier subsidies.

- **Carrier Models:** Carrier models are purchased through and tied to specific mobile service providers, often at a subsidized cost in exchange for agreeing to a service contract or installment payment plan. This option can make the initial purchase more affordable and sometimes includes carrier-specific perks or promotions, such as discounted service plans, free streaming subscriptions, or additional trade-in credit. Carrier models may come with pre-installed apps and services, and software updates might be delayed due to carrier testing and approval processes.

Additionally, switching carriers before fulfilling the contract terms may incur fees.

Financing and Trade-In Programs

- **Financing Programs:** Recognizing the premium price tag of the Galaxy S24 series, Samsung and many carriers offer financing options that allow customers to spread the cost of the device over a set period, typically 24 to 36 months. These programs often feature low or no interest, making them an attractive option for consumers who prefer not to pay the full price upfront. Financing through Samsung or a carrier usually requires a credit check and agreement to monthly payments, but it can make acquiring the latest technology more manageable financially.

- **Trade-In Programs:** To further offset the cost of the Galaxy S24 series, Samsung and carriers provide trade-in programs that offer credit for older devices toward the purchase of a new phone. The trade-in value depends on the model, age, and condition of the device being traded in. This option not only reduces the out-of-pocket expense for the new phone but also promotes the recycling and responsible disposal of electronic devices. Consumers considering a trade-in should evaluate the offered value against selling the old device independently, as sometimes the latter may yield a higher return.

In conclusion, the purchasing options for the Samsung Galaxy S24 series cater to a range of consumer preferences and financial situations. Whether opting for the flexibility of an unlocked model, the potential savings of a carrier model, the spread-out payments of financing, or the cost reduction of a trade-in program, there are multiple pathways to owning Samsung's latest flagship device. By carefully considering these options in the context of their needs, budget, and long-term mobile service plans, consumers can select the best approach to acquiring the Galaxy S24, S24+, or S24 Ultra.

CHAPTER 12

Pros and Cons

The Samsung Galaxy S24 series, comprising the S24, S24+, and S24 Ultra, brings a suite of features tailored to various user preferences and requirements. Each model within the series offers distinct advantages and disadvantages, making the choice highly dependent on individual needs, usage patterns, and budget considerations.

Advantages and Disadvantages of Each Model

Galaxy S24

- **Advantages:** The Galaxy S24, being the entry-level model of the series, offers solid performance with its latest chipset, a versatile camera system for everyday photography, and a compact design for easy handling and portability. It's priced more accessibly, making it a great option for users who want premium features without the premium price tag. The device also boasts a high-refresh-rate display for smooth scrolling and gaming experiences.

- **Disadvantages:** Compared to its more advanced siblings, the S24 has a smaller battery, which might not suit heavy users. The camera system, while capable, lacks the advanced zoom and high-resolution capabilities of the S24 Ultra. Additionally, the base model comes with less RAM and storage, which could be a limitation for power users.

Galaxy S24+

- **Advantages:** Building on the foundation of the S24, the S24+ model offers a larger display and battery, making it ideal for media consumption and longer usage between charges. It also includes slightly enhanced camera features over the base model, such as better low-light performance, providing a middle ground for users seeking upgrades without needing the top-tier specs of the Ultra.

- **Disadvantages:** The price increase from the S24 to the S24+ may not justify the incremental upgrades for all users. While it offers improvements, they may not be significant enough for those on a tight budget or users who prioritize compactness and portability over screen size.

Galaxy S24 Ultra

- **Advantages:** The Ultra model is the pinnacle of Samsung's flagship offerings, with a state-of-the-art camera system that includes a 200MP main sensor and unparalleled zoom capabilities. It features the largest screen and battery within the series, an enhanced S Pen for productivity, and up to 16GB of RAM for the ultimate performance. The S24 Ultra is designed for tech enthusiasts and power users who demand the best.

- Disadvantages: The high-end features of the S24 Ultra come with a premium price, making it the most expensive option in the series. Its large size may not appeal to users looking for a more compact device. Additionally, the advanced features may be overkill for average users, who might not utilize the device to its full potential, making it less cost-effective for them.

Which Model to Choose Based on Your Needs

Choosing the right model from the Galaxy S24 series depends on several factors, including how you use your phone, what features are most important to you, and your budget.

- For Everyday Users: If you're looking for a solid all-around smartphone that balances performance, camera quality, and price, the Galaxy S24 is an excellent choice. It offers the core features of the S24 series in a more compact and affordable package, suitable for everyday tasks, casual photography, and moderate media consumption.

- For Media Enthusiasts: If you prioritize screen real estate for watching videos, playing games, and browsing the web, along with a desire for a bit more battery life, the Galaxy S24+ is the ideal middle ground. It provides a larger display and battery than the base model, without the premium price of the Ultra.

- For Power Users and Photography Enthusiasts: Users who demand the highest performance, best camera capabilities, and maximum productivity features, including the S Pen, should consider the Galaxy S24 Ultra. It's tailored for users who use their phone as a primary device for photography, gaming, and productivity, offering top-of-the-line specs at a premium price.

In conclusion, the Samsung Galaxy S24 series caters to a broad spectrum of users, from casual to power users, with each model offering a tailored set of features and capabilities. By assessing your specific needs, usage patterns, and budget, you can select the model that best fits your lifestyle, ensuring you get the most value and satisfaction from your investment.

CHAPTER 13

Conclusion

The Samsung Galaxy S24 series represents a significant milestone in the evolution of mobile technology, embodying Samsung's commitment to innovation, quality, and user experience. With the introduction of the S24, S24+, and S24 Ultra, Samsung continues to push the boundaries of what's possible in a smartphone, catering to a diverse range of needs and preferences. As we reflect on the series and look forward to the future of Samsung Galaxy phones, several key points stand out.

Final Thoughts and Recommendations

The Galaxy S24 series impresses with its cutting-edge technology, refined design, and versatile capabilities. Each model in the series has been thoughtfully crafted to offer unique advantages, ensuring there's a suitable option for every type of user.

- **For the General User:** The Galaxy S24 provides a balance of performance, camera quality, and affordability, making it an excellent choice for most users. It offers the core Samsung flagship experience without unnecessary frills, suitable for day-to-day use, casual photography, and moderate media consumption.

- **For the Enthusiast:** The Galaxy S24+ strikes a perfect balance for users seeking enhancements in screen size, battery life, and camera performance without reaching into the premium price segment. It's ideal for media enthusiasts who value a larger display and longer usage between charges.

- **For the Power User:** The Galaxy S24 Ultra is the ultimate choice for tech enthusiasts and power users. Its unparalleled camera system, expansive display, superior performance, and S Pen functionality make it a powerhouse suited for professional photography, intensive gaming, and productivity tasks. While its premium price may be a consideration, the value it offers for its capabilities cannot be overstated.

Overall, the Samsung Galaxy S24 series stands out for its commitment to quality, innovation, and user satisfaction. When choosing between the models, consider your primary uses for the device, the features most important to you, and your budget. Regardless of which model you choose, the Galaxy S24 series is a testament to Samsung's leadership in the smartphone market, offering reliability, performance, and cutting-edge technology.

Future Outlook for Samsung Galaxy Phones

Looking ahead, the future of Samsung Galaxy phones is bright, with several trends and innovations on the horizon. Samsung's dedication to research and development suggests that future Galaxy phones will continue to lead in areas such as foldable technology, AI integration, sustainability, and connectivity.

- **Foldable Technology:** Samsung has already made significant strides in foldable devices, and future Galaxy phones are likely to further refine and popularize this technology, offering more durable, versatile, and affordable foldable options.

- **AI Integration:** Artificial intelligence will play an increasingly central role in enhancing the user experience, from camera functionality and battery management to personalized services and security features. Samsung's investments in AI suggest future Galaxy phones will be even smarter and more intuitive.

- **Sustainability:** As environmental concerns become more pressing, Samsung is likely to increase its focus on sustainability, using recycled materials, enhancing energy efficiency, and introducing more eco-friendly manufacturing processes.

- **Connectivity:** With the advent of 5G and beyond, future Galaxy phones will offer even faster, more reliable connectivity, supporting a wide range of new applications and services, from augmented reality experiences to seamless integration with the Internet of Things (IoT).

CHAPTER 14

Appendix

The Samsung Galaxy S24 series, with its advanced features and functionalities, is designed to deliver a premium smartphone experience. However, like any technology, users may encounter issues or seek ways to optimize their device's performance. This section offers guidance on troubleshooting common problems, extending battery life, and enhancing camera usage.

Troubleshooting Common Issues

- **Connectivity Problems:** If you're experiencing issues with Wi-Fi or Bluetooth connections, start by toggling the connectivity settings off and on. For persistent problems, forget the Wi-Fi network or unpair the Bluetooth device and reconnect. Restarting the phone can also resolve many connectivity issues.

- **Software Glitches:** Occasional software hiccups can often be resolved with a simple restart. If specific apps are causing issues, try clearing the app's cache or data from the settings menu. Ensure your device's software is up to date, as updates often include fixes for known issues.

- **Battery Drain:** Unusual battery drain can be due to rogue apps, excessive background data usage, or outdated software. Review battery usage in the device settings to identify and restrict high-consumption apps. Enabling power-saving modes can also mitigate battery drain issues.

- **Performance Lag:** If your Galaxy S24 starts to lag or becomes sluggish, check the storage space; a nearly full storage can impact performance. Consider deleting unnecessary files or using cloud storage services. Regularly restarting your device can also help maintain optimal performance.

How to Maximize Battery Life

- Adaptive Battery and Power Saving Modes: Utilize the adaptive battery feature to limit battery usage for infrequently used apps. Power saving modes can also extend your battery life by reducing background data usage and limiting performance for non-essential tasks.

- Screen Brightness and Refresh Rate: Lowering the screen brightness and reducing the refresh rate can significantly save battery life. Use the adaptive brightness feature for optimal screen visibility without excessive power consumption.

- Background Apps and Notifications: Restrict background usage for apps that don't need to run continuously. Disabling unnecessary notifications can also prevent apps from waking the device, thereby saving battery life.

- Network Settings: Turning off Wi-Fi, Bluetooth, and GPS when not in use can prevent these features from draining the battery. Use 5G selectively, as 5G connectivity consumes more power compared to 4G.

Tips for Getting the Most Out of Your Camera

- **Explore Pro Mode:** Take advantage of the Pro mode to gain full control over shutter speed, ISO, and white balance. This can significantly improve the quality of your photos, especially in challenging lighting conditions.

- **Utilize Night Mode:** The Night mode is designed to enhance low-light photography. It uses longer exposure times and AI stabilization to produce clear, bright photos in dark environments without a flash.

- **Experiment with Portrait Mode:** Use Portrait mode to achieve a beautiful bokeh effect, where the subject is in sharp focus against a softly blurred background. Adjusting the depth of field can enhance the overall impact of your portraits.

- Apply Filters and AR Features: Explore the camera's built-in filters and augmented reality features to add creativity to your shots. These tools can transform ordinary photos into artistic expressions or fun, shareable moments.

- Learn Composition Basics: Understanding basic photography principles such as the rule of thirds, leading lines, and framing can dramatically improve the composition of your photos, making them more visually appealing.

In summary, the Samsung Galaxy S24 series offers a comprehensive set of tools and features to tackle common issues, maximize battery life, and enhance camera functionality. By familiarizing themselves with these tips and practices, users can ensure their Galaxy S24 device operates smoothly, lasts longer between charges, and captures stunning photographs. Whether you're troubleshooting an issue, seeking to extend your battery life, or aiming to take your photography skills to the next level, these guidelines will help you get the most out of your Samsung Galaxy S24 series smartphone.

Detailed Answers To Frequently Asked Questions

Q: What are the key features of the Samsung Galaxy S24 Series?
A: The Samsung Galaxy S24 Series boasts several cutting-edge features, including improved camera capabilities, powerful processors, vibrant displays, and enhanced battery life. It also incorporates the latest software updates and innovations from Samsung.

Q: How many models are included in the Samsung Galaxy S24 Series?
A: The Samsung Galaxy S24 Series typically includes multiple models, such as the Galaxy S24, S24+, and S24 Ultra. Each model offers different screen sizes, camera configurations, and additional features to cater to various user preferences.

Q: What are the differences between the Galaxy S24, S24+, and S24 Ultra?
A: The main differences between these models usually lie in screen size, camera capabilities, battery capacity, and additional features. The Galaxy S24 Ultra typically offers the most advanced specifications and features compared to the other models in the series.

Q: Does the Samsung Galaxy S24 Series support

5G connectivity?

A: Yes, the Samsung Galaxy S24 Series is expected to support 5G connectivity, allowing users to experience faster data speeds and improved network performance, provided they have access to a 5G network.

Q: What improvements have been made to the camera system of the Samsung Galaxy S24 Series?

A: Samsung typically enhances the camera capabilities with each new Galaxy S series release. The Galaxy S24 Series may feature improved sensor technology, advanced image processing algorithms, and additional camera modes and features to enhance photography and videography experiences.

Q: What display technologies are used in the Samsung Galaxy S24 Series?

A: Samsung often incorporates high-quality AMOLED displays in its flagship Galaxy S series smartphones. These displays offer vibrant colors, deep blacks, and high contrast ratios, providing an immersive viewing experience for users.

Q: Is the Samsung Galaxy S24 Series water and dust resistant?

A: Yes, Samsung usually equips the Galaxy S24 Series with water and dust resistance, allowing the devices to withstand exposure to water and dust to a certain extent. However, it's essential to note the specific IP rating for each model to understand the level of protection provided.

Q: Does the Samsung Galaxy S24 Series support expandable storage?
A: Samsung typically offers models with different storage options, and some may support expandable storage via microSD cards. However, the availability of expandable storage may vary depending on the specific model and region.

Q: What software features are included in the Samsung Galaxy S24 Series?
A: The Samsung Galaxy S24 Series usually runs on the latest version of Samsung's One UI software, which is based on the Android operating system. This software typically includes various customization options, productivity features, security enhancements, and optimizations to improve overall performance and user experience.

Q: When will the Samsung Galaxy S24 Series be available for purchase?
A: The availability of the Samsung Galaxy S24 Series may vary depending on the region and market conditions. Samsung typically announces the release date during its official launch event, and the devices are usually available for purchase shortly after the announcement. It's recommended to check with official Samsung channels or authorized retailers for the most

accurate information regarding availability.

Q: What battery life can users expect from the Samsung Galaxy S24 Series?
A: The Samsung Galaxy S24 Series is designed with battery efficiency in mind, featuring large-capacity batteries and software optimizations to extend battery life. While actual battery life will depend on usage patterns and settings, users can expect improved battery performance compared to previous models. The Galaxy S24 Ultra typically offers the longest battery life due to its larger battery capacity.

Q: Are there any new color options available for the Samsung Galaxy S24 Series?
A: Samsung frequently updates the color options for its Galaxy S series to include both classic and trendy choices. The Galaxy S24 Series is expected to launch with a variety of colors, offering something for everyone's taste. Specific color options may vary by model and region.

Q: How does the Samsung Galaxy S24 Series integrate with other Samsung devices?
A: The Galaxy S24 Series is designed to seamlessly integrate with a wide range of Samsung devices, including tablets, laptops, and wearables. Features like Samsung DeX, which allows for a desktop-like experience by connecting the phone to a monitor, and Link to Windows, which integrates your phone's

functionalities with your Windows PC, enhance productivity and connectivity across devices.

Q: What security features are included in the Samsung Galaxy S24 Series?
A: Samsung places a high emphasis on security and privacy. The Galaxy S24 Series is equipped with Samsung Knox, a defense-grade security platform that protects your device from the chip level up. Additionally, it offers biometric authentication options, such as fingerprint scanning and facial recognition, to secure access to your device and personal data.

Q: Can the Samsung Galaxy S24 Series be used for mobile gaming?
A: Yes, the Galaxy S24 Series is well-suited for mobile gaming, thanks to its powerful processors, high-refresh-rate displays, and advanced cooling systems. These features ensure smooth gameplay and immersive experiences for a wide range of mobile games, from casual titles to more graphically intensive games.

Q: What is the price range for the Samsung Galaxy S24 Series?
A: Pricing for the Galaxy S24 Series will vary based on the model, storage capacity, and region. Typically, the Galaxy S24 and S24+ models are priced lower than the Galaxy S24 Ultra, which offers the most advanced features. Samsung usually announces specific pricing details during the launch event, and it's advisable to

check with official Samsung channels or authorized retailers for accurate pricing information.

Q: Does the Samsung Galaxy S24 Series offer any sustainability features?
A: Samsung is increasingly focusing on sustainability in its product designs and packaging. The Galaxy S24 Series may include eco-friendly materials, energy-efficient components, and recyclable packaging. Samsung's commitment to sustainability can also be seen in its efforts to reduce carbon emissions and support environmental initiatives.

Q: How can users customize their Samsung Galaxy S24 Series experience?
A: The Galaxy S24 Series runs on Samsung's One UI, which offers a wide range of customization options. Users can personalize their device with themes, icons, and always-on display settings. Additionally, users can adjust settings for enhanced productivity, such as edge panels and multitasking options, to tailor the device to their preferences and usage patterns.

Q: What warranty and support options are available for the Samsung Galaxy S24 Series?
A: Samsung typically offers a standard warranty for the Galaxy S24 Series, covering manufacturing defects and hardware issues for a specified period after purchase.

Extended warranty options and Samsung Care+ services may also be available for additional protection and support. It's recommended to review the warranty and support options provided in your region for detailed information.

Q: How does the Samsung Galaxy S24 Series contribute to an eco-friendly lifestyle?
A: Beyond using sustainable materials and packaging, the Samsung Galaxy S24 Series supports an eco-friendly lifestyle through software features that promote energy efficiency and reduce waste. Features such as adaptive battery and dark mode help conserve energy, while Samsung's trade-in and recycling programs encourage the responsible disposal and recycling of electronic devices.

www.ingramcontent.com/pod-product-compliance
Lightning Source LLC
LaVergne TN
LVHW051539050326
832903LV00033B/4324